THE THEOLOGIAN'S ENTERPRISE

AIDAN NICHOLS, O.P.

THE THEOLOGIAN'S ENTERPRISE

A Very Short Introduction

IGNATIUS PRESS   SAN FRANCISCO

Unless otherwise noted, the English translations of all papal documents have been taken from the Vatican website.

Cover design by Roxanne Mei Lum

© 2020 by Ignatius Press, San Francisco
All rights reserved
ISBN 978-1-62164-303-6 (PB)
ISBN 978-1-64229-109-4 (eBook)
Library of Congress Control Number 2019947844
Printed in the United States of America ∞

CONTENTS

Preface   7

An Initial Overview   9

1 What Is Theology?   13

2 Theology as Science and Wisdom   23

3 Theological Principles and Methods   37

4 The Sources of Theology   55

5 The Subject Matters of Theology   69

Conclusion   79

Bibliography   87

PREFACE

This study is a very short introduction to "the theologian's enterprise"—the concept and practice of Catholic theology. Despite its extreme concision, I believe it to be both comprehensive and deep. And, best of all, true.

Blackfriars, Cambridge
Memorial of Saint Fursey,
Abbot, 2018

AN INITIAL OVERVIEW

Here is an overview of this book.

Chapter 1 introduces the concept of theology which, in a key definition, it describes as the disciplined exploration of revelation. The distinction between natural and supernatural revelation produces in turn a distinction between natural and sacred theology, the difference between which turns on the act of faith. Through the preamble of faith, natural theology, whose object is God in creation and draws chiefly on metaphysics, transforms itself into sacred theology whose object is God in his saving outreach to man through (triune) personal self-disclosure, above all in the mysteries of the life of Christ with the Paschal Mystery, and its orientation to the final consummation, at their heart.

Chapter 2 considers the status of a theology as a science, linking together three key elements: theology as a science "subalternated" to God's own knowledge, theology as the taking of a unitary formal viewpoint, and theology as a circle of interconnected theses. Since theology is, however, a "tasting

9

science", which, through its relation with the mystical, has, in the theologian, direct contact with its own object, it must also be considered a wisdom. Theological wisdom is prepared by philosophical wisdom and, ideally, culminates as the wisdom of the saints. In any case, it is intrinsically linked to holiness and contemplation, and thus to the Liturgy and sacred aesthetics. Recognition of this linking makes possible the necessary balance between cataphatic or affirmative and apophatic or negative theology.

Chapter 3 looks at principles and methods in theology. It finds two essential principles: a philosophical principle of order and a theological principle of order, choice of which explains the plurality of Catholic theology, despite its simultaneous unity. Four key methods are identified: the analogy of being, the analogy of faith, totality thinking, and the method of convergence.

Chapter 4 investigates the sources of theology which are Scripture and Tradition. Critical tools for investigating the Bible are deemed to have a secondary importance compared with the specifically ecclesial manner of reading Scripture found in Tradition. The concept of Tradition is presented, and its "monuments" or expressions listed as the Fathers (and later Doctors), the liturgies and sacred iconography, creeds and councils, and the sense of the faithful as found in the lives of the saints and the works of piety. There are two aids to discernment in scanning these resources: Christian experience and the guidance of the contemporary Magisterium.

Chapter 5 looks at the various subject matters into which, through a process of specialization, theology has become (not altogether happily) subdivided. Four main subdivisions are recognized: fundamental theology, including apologetics; dogmatic theology, including both positive or historical theology (defined so as to include exegesis) and systematic or speculative theology; moral theology, understood as inclusive of spirituality (itself a synthesis of ascetical and mystical theology); and practical theology, which is here regarded as including pastoral theology and embracing all theological reflection on the mission of the Church to culture and society.

A conclusion summarises the theologian's enterprise by laying out the virtuous habits that the budding theologian must seek to acquire for his work if he is to do justice to the account of theology given in this book.

Finally, a bibliography is organized according to these chapters, with a section on each constituent theme for each chapter.

I

What Is Theology?

1.1 Theology is the disciplined exploration of revelation—that is, the self-disclosure of the divine. Such revelation exists in two modes: natural and supernatural.

1.1.1 *Natural revelation* takes place through the creation of the world. It is the disclosure of God through his work, the cosmos, of which man is the lynchpin, joining together in himself the physical and spiritual realms. Thanks to his crucial position, man can come to a grasp of finite being (material and intellectual) not only in itself but in its relation to its divine Source. The disciplined exploration of revelation in *this* mode is called "natural theology". Its resources are essentially those of metaphysics, but when integrated into systematics such natural theology benefits from the synthesis with the supernatural self-disclosure of God reflected in sacred theology. The latter yields illumination not otherwise available to the metaphysical intelligence.

1.1.2 The role of natural revelation is to dispose people for the reception of *supernatural revelation*. Revelation in this second mode comes about not through the universal structures of reality but through particular events in history as interpreted by those who participate in them as recipients, witnesses, or reflective rememberers. Revelation history is also called "salvation history" since the purpose of supernatural revelation is not simply to inform man about his true position in the cosmos but to bring him to his final destiny: beatitude as a sharing in the Creator's own intimate life. The events that make up salvation history are recorded in the Scriptures and relived in the worshipping life of the Church. So far from being a handicap, their particularity is essential to them, since they make use of the factor of *novelty* which differentiates man from other creatures whose life is determined exclusively by the natural rhythms of the cosmos. Events that are unforeseeable because they are not determined by the general course of the world, but rather, to the contrary, have the capacity to alter that course in some respect, may also be called *unique*, for they have a singularity which distinguishes them from naturally recurring patterns of life. This makes historical events highly suitable as vehicles for the inbreaking of supernatural revelation, which is not revelation through the world as a whole but a further—higher—mode of God's self-disclosure. Just as, moreover, historical events are not merely brute facts that, owing to their particularity, resist explanation by the generalizing approach of the life sciences, but, in addition, carry with them their own intelligibility, so likewise in the events that are the carriers of supernatural revelation, it is the role of the recipients, witnesses, and accredited rememberers to record, attest, and recall reflectively the interpretative *language* that accompanies the revelation events. So, particular events can vehicle the innovatory originality of divine action in the further mode of God's self-disclosure that is supernatural revelation. This is how *Dei verbum*, the Dogmatic Constitution of the Second Vatican Council on Divine Revelation (November 18, 1965), understands revelation: it happens as a synthesis of event and word.[1]

1.1.3 Natural theology's preparation of the way for the acceptance of supernatural revelation is called in Catholic theology the "preamble of faith". The *preamble of faith* considers three principal points: (1) how the divine Source of reality, God, if he really is infinite, can supplement the revelation of himself in nature; (2) how man, as the intelligent lynchpin of the cosmos, could receive such a further revelation if offered to him, and (3) how in history signs of supernatural revelation might be put in place through particular events—the particular events that are the key moments in the biblical narrative, defining by their significance the revelation history that comes about through Israel, in Jesus Christ (the culmination of the revelation to Israel), and (with Pentecost) by means of the Church Christ founded on the apostles.

1.1.4 The acceptance of supernatural revelation takes place through the *act of faith*. The act of faith is the objectively correct response to God's

[1] See *Dei verbum*, no. 2.

further self-revelation (over and above that found in natural revelation) in the particular events that define the history of Israel, Christ, and the Church. By following out the preamble of faith, the individual person judges these events to be worthy of his credence as bearers of a truth that goes beyond the truth available to metaphysics. By the act of faith, he assents with mind and heart to the claim of this further revelation, since, through a combination of emerging intuition and the help of divine grace as it illuminates the mind and attracts the will (or heart), the person apprehends in and through the signs set up by the revelatory events the definitive Good that will satisfy and more than satisfy his desires as it draws him to itself. The Eternal One manifests himself in historical events in such a way as not only to make his epiphany there but to alter time's course so that it flows (for the individual believer, but also for others) towards the eschaton, which is the world as consummated in God, and this is his beatitude (as it is theirs). Normal time, called in Greek "chronos", becomes a time of supernatural opportunity, called in Greek "kairos". By accepting the Gospel as carried by its appointed community, the apostolic Church, time opens out onto the realm of salvation, thus fulfilling the claim of revelation history to bring about man's abundant fulfillment in God.

1.1.5 This abundant fulfillment in God is achieved through *the mysteries of Christ's Incarnation and his Pasch* inasmuch as they make possible his final Parousia, whereby all the wounds of time find healing in the heavenly Jerusalem, married with earth (cf. Rev 21:2) in the nuptials of the Lamb and his Bride, the Church of the redeemed. There is a foretaste of this in the Liturgy of the Church. The natural inevitability of physical corruption, which haunts men with the fear of death, and the dominion of moral evil, which fills them with regret for the past, give way to the promised perfecting of their species. The mysteries of Christ, since they make this completion possible, and thus enable revelation history to reach its goal, occupy accordingly the central place in sacred theology.

1.2 The task of theology is to unpack what has just been asserted in the above. Its single most serviceable concept in so doing is that of *manifestation* which subsumes under itself theology's two most vital ideas. These two

ideas are *cause* and *sign*. The manifestation of
God—whether in creation or salvation—is the
causal impact of divine being brought to bear
on what is not God, either to constitute it, in
creation, or to heal and perfect it, in salvation.
At the same time, that causal impact of divine
being—either "on" nothing, in creation, or
on finite being, in salvation—sets up *the series
of signs* in which God signals to his creatures
and provides them with an understanding of
his nature and power (natural theology) as well
as his intimate life and tender plan for them
(revealed theology). Thus, theology is inescap-
ably both ontological (to do with divine being
in its agency) and hermeneutical (to do with
the interpretation of signs, both cosmological
and biblical). Any theology which fails to meet
these dual demands is a horse that falls at the
first hurdle. An example is "narrative theology" which, insofar as it takes its theological
principle of order from the salvation-history
structure of the biblical revelation, is herme-
neutically admirable, but by treating the cat-
egory of "story" as a substitute for ontology
narrative theology fails woefully in the provi-
sion of a philosophical principle of order to
accompany this.

1.3 Theology so understood is essentially *ecclesial* in character. Since the Church results from the divine causal impact in salvation history and because, as thus caused, she is the accredited interpreter of the signs which that history sets up, she alone can be the proper setting for revelation's disciplined exploration. Theology is, therefore, a quintessentially ecclesial practice. The chief vehicle for the communication of the tradition of faith to any individual person is Baptism, where the faith is handed over in its totality and which in the programme of the adult catechumenate takes place in the formal act of the *traditio symboli* (the "handing over of the Creed"). Like all the faithful, the theologian lives in the baptismal water. The theologian's act of faith, like that of every member of the Church, aims at full identification with the corporate act of faith of the Church as the Bride of Christ, his elected Covenant Partner. Any theology which departs from this ecclesial norm at once degenerates into esoteric pseudo-knowledge which is alien to Gospel truth. Though a theologian should strive in his thinking for beauty of form in the way he represents the apostolic deposit, he should do so precisely as service of the Church and homage to the Church's Lord—not as an attempt at "improvement" on the revelation divinely given. This gives theology an inner relation, not only to the Church as the Mystical Body and Beloved Bride of Christ, but also to the Church as a hierarchically ordered visible society. In responsible obedience to the Head, the Church from the beginning has sought to gather together the various expressions of the apostolic preaching (in the New Testament, for instance, the Synoptic Gospels as well as Saint Paul and Saint John) into that unity which the Fathers call the "rule of faith", *regula fidei*. At any given moment, the task of *bishops and pope* is to represent the rule of faith insofar as it is the point of unity of the believing consciousness of the Church. The rule of faith itself is found in Scripture as read in Tradition. Consequently, the contemporary Magisterium is at the service of revelation in its transmission. It is not itself a source for theology but a guide to the discernment of the sources (see chapter 4 below). The theologian's "role is to pursue in a particular way an ever deeper understanding of the Word of God found in the inspired Scriptures and handed on by the living Tradition of the Church. He does this in communion with the Magisterium which has been charged with the responsibility of preserving the deposit of faith."[2]

---

[2] Congregation for the Doctrine of the Faith, Instruction on the Ecclesial Vocation of the Theologian *Donum veritatis* (May 24, 1990), no. 6.

2

Theology as Science and Wisdom

2.1 Theology is a *science* inasmuch as (in a definition owed to Aristotle) it consists in certain knowledge by reference to the highest causes—and here there could be no higher cause, for this means, in theology's case, God in his loving plan for the world. Saint Thomas Aquinas describes theology as a "subalternated" science—that is, one which does not propose its own principles but receives those principles from elsewhere.[1] For its foundational axioms—which Thomas takes to be the articles of the Creed, themselves seen as summing up the Gospel as found in Scripture read in Tradition—theology depends on God's own knowledge of himself (and thus of his plan) and the knowledge which the saints enjoy of God (and of his plan which has been

[1] See Saint Thomas Aquinas, *Summa theologiae* I, q. 1, a. 2.

shared with the people of the redeemed, of
whom the saints are the perfected members).
Not surprisingly, theology is called therefore
sacra doctrina, "a *holy* teaching".

2.2 Moreover, it is typical of a science—a well-
formulated discipline—to have a *single formal
viewpoint* that makes possible a unitary overview
of the data or phenomena it considers. "Scientific" knowledge means adequately informed
understanding within the unity of a formal perspective. For theology, that perspective is God's
"take" on humanity-in-the-cosmos, from creation through salvation to final perfection in a
renewed world. Theology reflects revelation by
making its own revelation's overarching mas-
ter theme, which is God giving an account of
humanity in its relation to himself and his loving purpose—as these realities are disclosed climactically in the mysteries of the life of Christ
where God is made known as the Holy Trinity
in the same moment as there is disclosed the
character of our final consummation in God.
Theology's formal viewpoint is mimetic of revelation's own.

2.3 Theology is, more especially, a *systematically
ordered* science inasmuch as, when seeking to lay

out its contents derived by subalternation from God's own knowledge (and that of the blessed) through mimesis of revelation's own viewpoint on the world (see above 2.2), it presents its materials "encyclopaedically"—that is, in the form of a circle (in Greek, *kyklos*) of theses. Properly systematic theology constitutes a circle where the student may enter at *any* point on the circumference but at the same time needs to become acquainted with every point on the circumference in order to understand even his initial point of entry—whatever the latter may have been.[2] In other words, in scientific theology in its systematic form all aspects of revelation are explicitly related to each other and none can be fully understood without grasping all the rest. In this regard, systematics reflects the faith of the wider Church, where the same holds true as any properly constructed catechetical programme will attest.

2.4 Even when not fully systematic in the above sense, theology is always *scientia sapida*, a "tasting science". Owing to its relation to the act of faith, theology is defined not only by its

---

[2] See Aidan Nichols, O.P., *Chalice of God: A Systematic Theology in Outline* (Collegeville, MN: Liturgical Press, 2012).

scientific status but also through its *relation to the mystical*—namely, through contact with the very realities of which systematics speak: the mysteries themselves. Theology is *scientia sapida* because the theologian "tastes" his subject manner in the manner made possible by the mystical life, which for Thomist tradition is based on the fruitful reception of the gifts of the Holy Spirit given in principle to all at Christian initiation and more especially at chrismation (which the Latin Church calls "confirmation").[3] The effect of mystical grace in its impact on human powers is to orient the person more strongly to the inbreaking of supernatural revelation, above all through the mysteries of Christ in their relation to the eschatological goal of the Christian life at the Parousia. The theologian must be able to testify to the existential reverberation of Christian truth within the soul. Such appropriation of the revealed truth in one's own existence is why theology is fundamentally connected with holiness—and contemplation.

2.4.1 *Theology and holiness* are internally connected. Because prayer is for each person the chief

---

[3] See Ambroise Gareil, O.P., *Les dons du Saint-Esprit dans les saints dominicains* (Paris: Victor Lecofre, 1905).

precondition for the full opening of human faculties to the transformative work of God in human living, all theology must be praying theology. The loss of the sense that the great theologians were saints (for orthodoxy implies orthopraxy) results in an overintellectualising of the faith in which the spirit of adoration can vanish, and the set of faith-generated dispositions needed for theological sensibility weaken accordingly. Nearness to the hallowing Source is therefore crucial for the theological enterprise. According to Hans Urs von Balthasar, "Christian dogmatics must express the fact that the one whose thinking is dictated by faith is in a constant relationship of prayer with its object.... There is no such thing as a theological investigation that does not breathe the atmosphere of 'seeking in prayer'."[4] Not by chance does von Balthasar cite the person of Saint Thomas as an example of this fruitful union of knowledge and holy living. In commending Thomas as the classical theologian of the Latin Church, Pope Pius XI, making reference to his practice of abstinence and vigil as well as devotion to the image

---

[4] Hans Urs von Balthasar, "Theology and Sanctity", in *Explorations in Theology*, vol. 1, *The Word Made Flesh* (San Francisco: Ignatius Press, 1989), pp. 206–7.

of the Crucified, concluded that "humility then and cleanness of heart together with unflagging zeal for prayer made the soul of Thomas [in his theological work] docile and ready to yield to the promptings and illuminations of the Holy Ghost."[5]

2.4.2 *Theology and contemplation* are equally bonded together in holy living. The practice of contemplation is an indispensable propaedeutic for hearing responsively to the Word of God, for the way in which sanctification becomes theological reflection passes over the bridge of contemplation. For this reason, all theology must learn more specifically from the characteristically monastic mode of theological practice, of which Saint Bernard is the emblematic figure.[6] We have to be enraptured and taken out of ourselves towards the Beloved by experiencing the fascination of God's self-revelation in the call it sends out to man. By a monasticism of the heart, every theologian needs to replicate this attitude. No theologian can dispense

[5] Pius XI, *Studiorum ducem* (London: Catholic Truth Society, 1923), p. 5.

[6] See Etienne Gilson, *The Mystical Theology of St. Bernard* (London: Sheed and Ward, 1940).

with the experience of living out the dogmas of the Church in the individual soul as it journeys towards God.

2.4.3 The contemplative factor in theology implies in turn theology's *relation to the Liturgy* in which the understanding of the Creed, the summation of Scripture, is lived "doxologically" by Christ's faithful people. The baptized person, initiated into the Christian mystery, then goes on to be built up in the faith by the Liturgy which presents him with the *phronema ekklesiastikon*, the "deep mind of the Church", thus conveying the *sensus catholicus*, the "Catholic sense", and stimulating in return a praise-filled, giving glory to God. The interrelation of theology with the life of prayer cannot be restricted to personal contemplation but must embrace as well the role of liturgical prayer in the theological task. "That is why the altar and the theologian's cell—his workspace—must be conjoined. The deepest origins of the theologian's inspiration must be nourished from the altar."[7] Like the Liturgy, the theologian comes to the Father

---

[7] Sergei Bulgakov, "Dogma and Dogmatic Theology", in *Tradition Alive*, ed. Michael Plekon (Lanham, MD: Bowman and Littlefield, 2003), p. 69; see pp. 67–80.

through the Son and the Spirit. In that Liturgy the Church is disclosed as the Bride of the Lamb calling out with the Spirit for the coming Lord, in the presence of the Mother of God and the saints. Habitual recourse to this setting, with its nuptial relation to Christ, its eschatological orientation, and its recognition of the intercessory value of the communion of saints as the wider human context of theological practice, is normative for theological endeavour.

2.4.4 From this there follows the *relation of theology to aesthetics*, for what is given to the saint (the normative Christian) in the contemplation that the Liturgy, above all, makes possible is a superabounding life and truth that calls forth the cry "It is wonderful!", and this "cry" represents the fundamental aesthetic response to existence. There is necessarily, then, an aesthetics of the theological task. The theologian has not only to consider God as Truth, the supremely real, upholding all true states of affairs by his creative power, nor simply to approach him as the supreme Good, integrating in himself all the partial goods sought by rational creatures. The theologian has also to desire God as the consummate Beauty, who even now can be contemplated in the radiant figuration of the mysteries, climactically in the Paschal Mystery of the Incarnate Word. He who reveals himself in the supernatural mode is not simply the *Qui est*, the Source of all being, or the *Summum Bonum*, the highest good, but the One who through his beauty inspires us with the longing of love, a love that shapes all we do, so that the objectively true and the morally good are united in pursuit of Beauty himself. The *sapida scientia* of theology must bear witness by its own form to the divine glory.[8] Thus, theology will learn not only verbally, from other writings, but also visually, from the Church's *icons*, which can be beautifully vivid, imaginatively deep, expressively vital, and sublimely transformative. They can provocatively question us by drawing attention to the realities of sin and suffering, evoke surprise, communicate meditative stillness, and in all these ways assist the prayerful and contemplative appropriation of revelation that is modelled in the sacred Liturgy as a whole.

2.5 Theology is described by the Church's divines, not simply as a science, but also as a *wisdom*.

[8] Cf. Hans Urs von Balthasar, *The Glory of the Lord: A Theological Aesthetics*, vol. 1, *Seeing the Form* (San Francisco: Ignatius Press, 1982).

And indeed theology has a *sophianic* character. Divine Wisdom has two faces. One of them is God's own, and it is turned towards the world, and the other is the world's, and this is a created mode of the divine Wisdom invested in finite being so as to enable the world to turn towards God. The Uncreated Wisdom of God, in founding the creation, embodied within it a created wisdom that man can make his own, which he can do either through his own native faculties, where natural revelation is in question, or, when the mysteries of supernatural revelation are involved, by grace. This sophianic foundation for the human response to God in both natural and engraced ways is reflected in the ways in which human understanding can take *wisdom form*. We customarily distinguish between three wisdoms.

2.5.1 Sacred theology contains within itself a philosophical component—the *philosophica perennis*, a truthful, sane-making, and life-enhancing metaphysic, which is *already a wisdom*, at the level of the natural creation, for it is objectively attuned to the divine Wisdom of the Creator.

2.5.2 But thanks to the *sapida scientia* character it derives from correspondence with God's revelatory action, sacred theology is itself such wisdom *in heightened form*. The theology that takes its rise from the mysteries of Christ in their orientation to the eschaton has resources unavailable to philosophy as such, and these furnish a foretaste of the glorious transformation at the end of time by which man in his cosmic setting will be brought to his perfection. Though attaining man in all that he is, in his moral, cultural, and social activities, sacred theology, being rooted in the life of God in his loving outreach to man, extends beyond these to his final end.

2.5.3 The *wisdom of the saints*, which presupposes the shaping of their minds and hearts by the saving revelation, is not only intrinsically related (accordingly) to theological wisdom. More than this, as the intimate infusion of the gift of Wisdom into human powers elevated by grace through the mysteries, it is the supreme flowering of Christian wisdom. "By means of the wisdom which is acquired by human study, we have a right judgment about divine things according to the perfect use of reason. But there is another wisdom that comes down from above and judges of divine things by virtue of the natural affinity it has with them. This is the gift of the Holy Ghost ... by which a man is made perfect in divine things, not only learning but also experiencing divine things."[9]

2.5.4 These three wisdoms make up an *ordered sequence*. Philosophical wisdom is ultimately ordered to theological wisdom just as theological wisdom is ultimately ordered to the infused wisdom of the saints. Thus, the rigorous discourse of philosophy is, even at the natural level, an instrument for making progress in intellectual light, since reason, whether analytic or constructive, is ultimately in the service of the simple looking to the real that is intellectual vision. When wisdom is supernaturalised through divine revelation, such looking, under the impact of the gifts of the Holy Spirit, can take the form of an immediate union with God and an anticipation of the perfect connubiality of the Lord with his Church in the age to come.

2.5.5 When theology reaches its own ideal as wisdom it finds at once the proper balance between the *cataphatic* (the affirmative voice)

---

[9] *Summa theologiae* I-II q. 45, a. 1 ad 2.

and the *apophatic* (the negative voice), which is determinative for its discourse. Theology must be audacious in its claims, for it is, thanks to its correspondence with God's self-revelation, essentially cataphatic, given to making affirmations about God and his design. Yet, this audacity must be tempered by an awareness of its own limits, for theology is also apophatic, acknowledging the way God and the future glory he holds out to man exceed all human concepts, such that theology itself will point to the appropriateness of silent adoration of what these affirmations portend. God exceeds all knowledge and all the perfections whereby we speak of him as the True, the Good, and the Beautiful—first and foremost in him before, in derivative and fragmentary ways, they are in creatures according to their proper mode. The only actual perfections that lie within our range are those presented by sensuous things, and these are themselves participations—real if enfeebled—in him of whom we are concerned with knowing. The "silence of Saint Thomas", his apophaticism, derived from the Fathers, and notably from Saint Augustine and Denys the Areopagite, informed as their thought was by the Platonic school, is, however, balanced cataphatically by the evangelical proclamation, by the apostolic tradition, and by the experience of salvation lived in the Church, especially in prayer and sacrament.

3

Theological Principles and Methods

3.1 We have said that theology is the disciplined exploration of revelation. What does such disciplined exploration involve? As to *principles*, it entails the scanning of the sources of revelation with the help of two "principles of order".

3.1.1 Such scanning requires in the first place the choice of a *philosophical principle of order* in theology. Theology must make use of a sound philosophy, for without a right understanding of basic realities in the created order the affirmations of theology about divine revelation can be undermined. And if philosophy cannot show that human minds can grasp transcendent truth, the ability of theology to make its assertions heard will be undermined likewise.

3.1.1.1 The *optimism of the Church that such a philosophy is available* is based more on Christian anthropology than on epistemology simply as such. She holds that humans are not only God's creatures but are made in the image of God, that they are destined for God and have received accordingly a capacity for participating in the journey towards God which will include their own characteristic activity. For as Pope Saint John Paul II has stated, "Faith and reason are like two wings on which the human spirit rises to the contemplation of truth; and God has placed in the human heart a desire to know the truth—in a word, to know God himself—so that, by knowing and loving God, men and women may also come to the fullness of truth about themselves."[1] Philosophically expressed, the knowledge in human minds *derives* from sensuous things, but that knowledge is not, however, sensuously *possessed*. There is in man a natural intellectual light—namely, reason itself—which is a participation in, and a resemblance to, the divine light. In conserving the human being in existence, God

---

[1] John Paul II, encyclical letter *Fides et ratio* (September 14, 1998), Preamble.

sustains the mind and its natural light. In this way the human person is indebted to God for all his intellectual operations. These convictions produce a marked bias against epistemic reductionism in all its forms.

3.1.1.2 A philosophy suited to theology's needs will, accordingly, carry out the *negative task* of excluding common errors in this regard. In *Aeterni patris* (August 4, 1879), Leo XIII warned against scepticism and rationalism; in *Humani generis* (August 12, 1950), Pius XII cautioned against evolutionism, existentialism, and historicism; and in *Fides et ratio* (September 14, 1998), John Paul II extended this list by adding to it radical phenomenalism, relativism, eclecticism, scientism, pragmatism, and nihilism.

3.1.1.3 A philosophy suited to theology must also *serve positively* theology's needs. Three criteria may be suggested for the aims of a philosophy congruent with revelation.[2] A philosophy that can aid theology must have a sapiential character, able to articulate the question of the meaning of life and to unify knowledge within a

---

[2] Cf. ibid., nos. 81–83.

coherent framework to that end. It must also present the objectivity of truth wherein mind and the real are "adequated" to each other. Lastly, it must have a full metaphysical range, reaching out beyond the empirical to truth that is foundational and ultimate. Only so can philosophy be adequate as a natural wisdom that can serve as handmaid to the revealed wisdom of sacred theology.

3.1.1.4 The *philosophy of Saint Thomas* proves an exemplary model of all this. His philosophy is admirably congruent with sacred doctrine, and if sacred doctrine is true, then his philosophy can be deemed highly suitable for the interpretation of experience at large, as well as for restoring the unity of culture under the aegis of faith. At the heart of Thomas' philosophy lies a governing intuition, subsequently unfolded in a net of concepts. For this intuition, universal being is an immense outpouring from a Source, a gigantic cascade that forms the cosmos in the graded reality of things, from atoms to archangels. The Source operates like a sun projecting its waves so as to constitute a world of light. The symbol of light occurs very frequently in Aquinas so as to express at once the objectivity

of being and also its subjective state in knowing.
Being which is light is also idea—that is, also
knowing, since the fuller the being is, the more
transparent it is to itself. Thomist metaphysics
hails God by the name he revealed to Moses at
the Burning Bush (Ex 3:14): God is "I AM WHO
I AM." The God whom this formula defines precisely by not defining him contains virtually and
eminently all that is finite—including even that
which escapes all definition since it falls short
of it rather than exceeding it—namely, sheer
matter. God as the Primal Actuality who is also
the First Intelligible is the Source of all being as
of all ideas. In the celebrated Five Ways, Saint
Thomas, starting now not from this intuition
but from *the real in its concreteness*, shows how
the need to explain existence can only be satis-
fied by postulating God in just such terms. The
real is thus unified in God, but it is not for that
reason the less genuinely plural. Here, Thomas'
thought makes a crucial breakthrough in the-
istic metaphysics. "The God of Saint Thomas
is essentially Being in its absolute infinity; and
because he is existence itself, he can give it to
others, that is to say, he can create ... an order
of active and, eventually, of free causes, each of
which bears witness to the infinite generosity

of its author."[3] Created causes cannot create, but they can and do have an efficiency of their own. This is part and parcel of the way God imparts to creatures something of his own perfection so far as they can receive it. Thus, through the movement of causality the world exhibits traces of the generosity of its Creator. This is the *fundamental outline of natural revelation* which must be factored into all revealed theology.

3.1.1.5 We should also note, with Pope Pius XII, that the philosophy of Thomas, or more widely the *philosophia perennis*, can and should be *enriched and amplified* by other currents of philosophical thought insofar as these have identified genuine elements of truth.[4] Thus supplemented, sacred theology can find in the philosophy of Thomas the ideal *philosophical principle of order in theology*.

3.1.1.6 The relation of philosophy to theology and more widely of reason to faith is isometric with *the relation of nature to grace*. Reason lies open to accepting from revelation truths that lie at the limits of its own capacity to generate

[3] Etienne Gilson, *Saint Thomas Aquinas* (London: British Academy, 1932), p. 10.
[4] See Pius XII, encyclical letter *Humani generis* (August 12, 1950), no. 9.

(but whose congruence with its scanning of the world it can acknowledge) only because nature lies inherently open to grace, though having its own identity vis-à-vis grace. Getting the relation of nature and grace right is, accordingly, very important for Catholic thought. There are natural structures still intact within the totality of the Christian person and the Christian city. Yet as Chesterton wrote in *The Everlasting Man*, nature is "always looking for the supermatural".[5] There is a natural desire for God—a "receptive readiness" for him which may be thought of as "rooted in the fact of having already been given the gift of *esse* absolutely gratis".[6] The gift of being renders existence a receptacle for fresh influxes from divine resources.

3.1.2 After a philosophical principle of order there is need to elect a *theological principle of order* likewise. This forms the second constitutive principle in theology. Thus, for example, for his *Summa theologiae*, Saint Thomas selected a theological

[5] G. K. Chesterton, *The Everlasting Man* (London: Hodder and Stoughton, 1927), p. 150.
[6] Nicholas Healy, "Henri de Lubac on Nature and Grace: A Note on Some Recent Contributions to the Debate", *Communio* 35 (2008): 547; see pp. 535–64.

principle of order that sees the creation as coming forth *from* God and *returning* to him, which in the crucial case of man takes the form of the moral, ascetical, and spiritual life—and does so thanks to the Incarnation and the Paschal Mystery, since Jesus Christ, as the Saviour of man, is the *via ad Deum*, "the way to God". In the present writer's outline systematics, *Chalice of God*,[7] the theological principle of order chosen is *the plenary outpouring of divine life in grace and glory*, seen as filling up the "receptacle" of the natural creation, above all in man. The fulfilling and superfulfilling of the world's possibilities comes about through the Christological determination of history, whose transforming power, ordered to the entry of creation into the life of the Trinity, has its effect as the mysteries of Christ are transposed into the pattern of sacramental living in the Church. It should be noted that no one theological principle of order can do justice to the entirety of revelation, which is too full in its span to submit to a single interpretative scheme. Nevertheless, each theology should aim asymptotically at representing that fullness.

---

[7] Aidan Nichols, O.P., *Chalice of God: A Systematic Theology in Outline* (Collegeville, MN: Liturgical Press, 2012).

3.1.3 The variety of possible theological principles of order is what explains the *simultaneous unity and plurality* of Catholic theology. The unity of holy teaching is established by the nature of revelation itself, as transmitted in the Church—and on the presupposition that the theologian approaches his task in the properly ecclesial manner described above. The plurality of particular theologies derives from the spectrum of possibilities created by the concept of a theological ordering principle—and this testifies to the abundant richness of revelation in its own right. This plurality may also be linked to the selection of a philosophical principle of order, though the same philosophical principle of order, derived from a just view of natural reality, can coexist happily with different theological principles of ordering the materials of supernatural revelation. Thus, the two examples of a theological principle of order given above presume a quasi-identical body of philosophical convictions.

3.2 As to *methods*, a theology which has established its philosophical and theological principles of order will do well to employ in addition *four specific methods*. These are the analogy of being, the analogy of faith, totality thinking, and convergence thinking. Each must now be considered in turn.

3.2.1 *Analogia entis*, the "analogy of being", is crucial to the metaphysical underpinning of revealed theology—and is especially well exhibited in the philosophical principle of order recommended above. Without the ability to articulate the relation of God to creatures in ontological terms, we shall not be able to describe the nature of the manifestation God makes of himself in supernatural revelation in saving history: not the character of manifestation as causal impact nor the bearing of manifestation as a series of signs. The word "analogy" refers in the first place to the language in which ontology is expressed. Analogous predication holds a middle position between univocal and equivocal predication. Its terms indicate both likeness and difference in specifiable respects, whereas "univocity" connotes likeness alone, and "equivocation" only difference. More searchingly, however, "analogy" concerns the character of being itself, which possesses unity when considered in its Source, yet plurality when considered in the variety of beings that derive from that Source, and thus is both like its Source and also different from it. Thus, the ontology subjacent to analogy gives rise to the language of analogy. The God who is *indescribable* inasmuch as he is not found among the categories of worldly being, since utterly different from them, can nevertheless be *spoken of*, thanks to the world's relation to him by virtue of creation, through which the world is like him in certain respects. Moreover, as the Source who draws finite being from nothing, he is immediately present to all things and so can exercise causal power in their regard, not just in general, for the governance of the cosmos, but also for the specific goal of human salvation. And as absolutely plenary Being, since all perfections are his in a simultaneous simplicity, such that his Wisdom is fully comprehensive, God is able to oversee all creation and its history, and so set up, through particular events, the sign system that renders revelation possible and intelligible. The theologian's ability to speak analogically of God on the basis of the *analogia entis* is, accordingly, a presupposition of the key theological idea of *manifestation* (as both cause and sign). More widely still, the analogy of being—whereby the whole of reality, thanks to its matrix in the divine Source, is a single

interconnected web—makes possible the illumination of one particular reality by reference
to others. This is never more important than
when we are dealing with the unique events in
which the saving revelation is manifested, since,
in order to interpret them well, maximizing the
resources of possible comparison is highly desirable. According to von Balthasar, "There is a
real science of the (relatively or wholly) unique
event even when this unique object is only to
be circled round and expressed with the instru-
ments of various analogies."[8]

3.2.2 The second desirable method to be used
within the overall context of the philosophical
and theological principles of order is the *analogy
of faith*, which seeks to lay out the inner coherence between the various doctrines deriving
from the revelatory totality, and in this way to
exhibit the "connexion of the mysteries"—in
the helpful, indeed indispensable, phrase put
forward by the First Vatican Council in its
Dogmatic Constitution on Faith *Dei filius*.[9] All
aspects of revelation are interconnected in the

---

[8] Hans Urs von Balthasar, *Convergences: To the Source of the Christian Mystery* (San Francisco: Ignatius Press, 1982), p. 51.

[9] *Dei filius* (April 24, 1870), chap. 4, no. 4.

overarching beauty of the divine plan and in relation to the archetypal Beauty of the divine Planner. Just as it is a philosophical imperative to find coherence between truth claims, so it is a theological imperative to show how all the different theses which revelation underpins *belong together in a unitary whole*. None of the various treatises that make up the different subject matters of theology can be dealt with in isolation. All must be interrelated—which is why the greatest theological masters have typically avoided the production of separate theological treatises (examples from the thirteenth and nineteenth centuries, respectively, are Saint Thomas and Matthias Joseph Scheeben) and found instead other genres of writing that by their literary form are better able to express the analogy of faith.

3.2.3 The need for totality thinking is already indicated by the analogy of faith. But the *totality method* does not simply reiterate the imperative to interlink the contents of revelation once given theological form. Rather, it draws attention to the theologian's task of *linking the theological theses to all other knowledge*, whether theoretical or practical. Since divine revelation is the greatest truth, goodness, and beauty that can be known, all other truth (theoretical knowledge, in philosophy or the sciences), goodness, and beauty (practical knowledge in morals and art) can and should be brought, therefore, into organic relationship with sacred theology.

3.2.4 If poorly handled (notably in the context of an ill-chosen philosophical or theological principle of order), the use of totality thinking might lead to a distancing of theology from its own centre—the mysteries of the Incarnation and the Pasch with their orientation to the eschaton. Liberation theology, with a weak philosophical principle of order drawn from sociology, and a deficient theological principle of order taken from a biblical messianism that is temporally (mis-)understood, is an obvious example. Hence, among theological methods we must also count what von Balthasar's theology, at least in Anglophone form, calls *convergence* thinking.[10] There is a constant need in theology to home in on the centre of the sacred teaching, to return time and again to the central mysteries of faith. This should not

[10] Von Balthasar, *Convergences*.

be done, however, by paring down the wealth of revelation, either in its internal coherence, as scanned theologically by the analogy of faith, or in its overall comprehensiveness, as reflected in the relations theology establishes with other disciplines in totality thinking, such that only bare essentials are left. Rather, the convergence method will have as its aim *to manifest that same revelatory wealth's abiding source*. Behind theological faith in its full amplitude, understood both *ad intra* (in the manner of the analogy of faith) and *ad extra* (in the manner of totality thinking), lies the uniqueness of God's self-revelation in the climactic event of the Pasch of the Incarnate Word in his reconciling man to God and summing up the entire cosmos in himself as its new and abiding centre. Thus, in von Balthasar's theology the keynote of convergence thinking is defined as the "divine crucified incarnate love".[11]

3.3 Such convergence thinking presents us with *theologia prima*, "prime theology", which is doxological contemplation of the revelatory centre, the God-Man in his death and Resurrection

[11] Ibid., p. 12.

leading to the glorifying of God's grace by hearers of the Word who will henceforth live theocentrically, in the fashion of true wisdom, and thus by a manner of life attuned to the Father's gift of himself to man in his Son—which makes theirs a charitable life opening onto the needs of the brother or sister. This *prima theologia*, which through being doxologically contemplative is also (in the manner just outlined) sapiential and existential, alone corresponds fully to the requirements for sacred theology set out in chapter 1 above.

3.3.1 But *theologia prima* goes on to generate two important secondary forms of theology: the "apologetics" or *dialectical theology* which take the unbeliever, or the follower of some other religion, as its interlocutor in a "Court of the Gentiles" or in interreligious dialogue, and the "kerygmatics" or *theology of proclamation* which attunes the central message of *prima theologia* to specific cultures, thus enhancing the evangelical power both of the primary theology itself and of the first of the two secondary theologies, dialectical theology or apologetics.

3.3.2 An example of such an "*inculturated*" theology would be in England the use of John Henry

Newman's distinctive theological approaches considered as a *via anglica*, or "English Way".[12] Newman's familiarity with the mores, history, literature, and institutions that make up English life enabled him to present Catholic Christianity with a persuasiveness to his fellow countrymen that exceeded the reach of the various Scholasticisms of his time. Newman combined the empiricism engendered in the English by their early exposure to the scientific revolution (a respect for facts expressed in Newman's apologetics, which turns on the accumulation of probabilities, and in his account of doctrinal development with its close attention to the historical process) with the transcendentalism retained from the Romantic Movement (and embodied in Newman's robust language about the invisible world which forms the wider setting of human existence); he seasoned both with a personal individualism (notably in his doctrine of conscience) congenial to a nation that dislikes collectivism and favours eccentrics. He thus indicated a way forward for a Catholic strategy in English culture

[12] See John Coulson and A. M. Allchin, ed., *The Rediscovery of Newman: An Oxford Symposium* (London: Sheed and Ward and Society for the Promotion of Christian Knowledge, 1967), and J. H. Walgrave, O.P., *Newman the Theologian: The Nature of Belief and Doctrine as Exemplified in His Life and Works* (London: Geoffrey Chapman, 1960).

and was appropriately chosen by Pope Benedict XVI as the patron of the "Ordinariate of Our Lady of Walsingham", intended as the normal means whereby in the future English Anglicans who wish to enter into communion with the See of Peter may enter the Catholic Church.

4

The Sources of Theology

4.1 Identification of the sources of theology follows from what has been said about the nature of theology as discussed in chapter 1. Since theology is a disciplined exploration of the revelation transmitted in Scripture in the Church—and hence in Tradition—the *Bible* and the various monuments of *Tradition* will be its accredited sources.

4.2.1 *Scripture* comes first. Thus, Saint Thomas would have seen himself first and foremost as a commentator on Scripture and not just in his formally biblical works. All tools for studying the Bible that can throw light on the meaning of the sacred text are worth employing. That will mean, then, philological study, through familiarity with the original languages; the study of textual criticism, which concerns the establishing of the best text from a range of variants; investigation of ancient history, which gives entry to the world of the periods when Scripture was written; and also the various approaches to the biblical texts that bear, compendiously, the name of the "historical" or "historical-critical" method. To these may be added such subsequent extensions of critical method in biblical study as "structuralist" exegesis and "reader-reception" theory, both of which differ from the historical-critical method in their comparative indifference to history as such but resemble it inasmuch as they are literary methods originally applied to secular—that is, extrarevelatory—texts (those not produced by participants, witnesses, or accredited rememberers of the revelation events), and now transferred by academic students to the biblical corpus. These tools, though capable of giving insight into the texts (in various degrees), are none of them at the level of the Church's own reading of Scripture as found in Tradition.

4.2.2 The Church has her own exegetical approach which entails, firstly, as the example of the Fathers and the Liturgy shows, the *Christocentric* *reading of the Scriptures as a whole.* This approach alone is consonant with sound theological method which by convergence thinking centres sacred doctrine on the heart of the mysteries. By following the Church's own exegetical manner, it is possible to confirm how theology is rightly Christ-centred since Scripture thus read in Tradition emerges as giving access to the revelatory fullness, which is Jesus Christ, the form at once of God (he is the Trinitarian Son) and of man (he is the second and true Adam), and thus the form of the God-Man relation (for both natures, divine and human are personally united in him) in which that relation receives its norm. *Ressourcement*, going back to the sources, is useless without *recentrement*, recentering on Christ as the manifestation of the Holy Trinity in a human way. Christ is the centre of the Scriptures, and it is because Scripture is *not its own centre* that the many innerbiblical theologies (compare the Synoptics, Saint Paul, Saint John) can coexist without detriment to its coherence, and the even more numerous extrabiblical theologies (I have mentioned notably Saint Thomas', and that of von Balthasar) can come to be, in the service of ecclesial thought, without jeopardizing Scripture's originality.

4.2.3 Here, some reference to the biblical *canon* is essential. The biblical canon serves the Holy Spirit as a vehicle for his actualizing the total historical form of the revelation of salvation. The Holy Spirit puts the canon to use by transforming the Old Testament Christologically through unifying it with the New. Christians should not practise exegesis of the elder Testament as though they were Jews. The Holy Spirit also uses the canon of Scripture by transposing the literal sense of both the Old Testament and the New into that spiritual sense which is the Christ event as life-giving for the members of the Church as a whole. That means, Christians should never practise exegesis as though they were not believers at all. Exegesis is concerned with what the message of the Bible means for the "I" of the Church, for a Christian is such only in the Church and through her. The Church does not take her understanding of biblical revelation from the academy, but receives an overall grasp of it, imprinted in her heart, by the way the Holy Spirit brings to life what she heard from the lips of Christ and the apostles. She interprets the Scriptures with the assistance of the Holy Spirit by whose aid, through the charism of inspiration, and its consequence in inerrancy, the biblical writers contributed to the canon.

4.2.4 Thus, the *historical-critical method* of reading Scripture, for all its value in giving historical vividness to the texts in their original contexts, cannot as such be determinative for Catholic theology. The same is true for all other naturally conceived methods of biblical study which depend on the (false) presupposition that this literature is no more unique than any other. But, thanks to its relation to revelation, it is in a class all its own. Thus were theology left without recourse beyond the text as researched by natural methods, it would necessarily be underdetermined in its reading of Scripture. A supplement is, however, available, since the dogmatic meaning of Scripture is found in Tradition, and therefore in a fashion not accessible to philologists or historians *as such*.

4.3 *Tradition* is to be thought of as both a content and a process or event. First of all, it is a content, a "deposit"—a banal-sounding term, but one must think not of paying a week's earnings into the bank but, rather, of a priceless treasury. As the Dogmatic Constitution of the

Second Vatican Council on Divine Revelation puts it, "Sacred Tradition and Sacred Scripture make up a single sacred deposit of the Word of God".[1] But, of its nature this deposit requires to be transmitted across the generations, for *traditio* is also a process, the active transmission of the Word of God found as deposit, the sharing of a treasure across time. Tradition is the doctrine of faith as handed down in a way inseparable from the communication of the liturgical rites whose ultimate impulse is Pentecost. Tradition indeed would include the Scriptures, were we not to add, to distinguish Tradition from Scripture, the phrase "by word of mouth", by which is meant *by some means other than writing*. Saint Paul congratulates the Corinthians for "maintain[ing] the traditions even as I delivered them to you" (1 Cor 11:2), the "order of tradition [that the apostles] have transmitted to those to whom they entrusted the churches".[2] The faith of the Church is possessed globally in the milieu which the apostles created to be the matrix of a continuing transmission of the life and truth of the Gospel. Though no point of belief may

---

[1] *Dei verbum* (November 18, 1965), no. 10.
[2] Saint Irenaeus, *Against the Heresies* III.4.1.

depend on Tradition exclusive of all reference
to Scripture, at the same time no point of belief
turns on Scripture alone without reference to
Tradition so understood; for in the Tradition-
borne ecclesial life where Scripture alone is
properly read, the deposit is elaborated by being
lived, defended, and explained by the faithful
over time, thus producing its "monuments" or
concrete embodiments. The question thus arises
of what those monuments are.

4.3.1 The first is the witness of the *Fathers of the
Church*. The Christ-centred exegesis of Scripture described above is how the Fathers pro-
ceeded, but the Fathers are normative for sacred
theology, not only in this but in *the entire way in
which they passed on the apostolic faith*. The revelation given to the apostles is not fully received
in the wider Church until it enters the minds
and hearts of the Fathers, who are its authoritative "professional rememberers". They were
able to register and promote revelation in its
unity and wholeness through three main media:
(1) their preaching and (other) writing, (2) the
creeds they formulated, and (3) the liturgies
they devised. They remain in their "consensus"
an abiding reference point for all subsequent

Catholic theology. Acquaintance with the Fathers is therefore a *sine qua non* for every theologian who needs to make sustained reference to them in his work. This is not only because of their unique standing as the corporate recipient of the apostolic preaching in its authoritative credal, liturgical, and wider theological form, but owing to the ethos of their testimony to the faith. The Fathers embody the "identikit" picture of a theologian offered in the description of theology as wisdom in chapter 2. So it is fortunate that the works of the Fathers, whether Greek, Latin, or Syriac, are increasingly available in English translations as well as in scholarly editions in the original languages.

4.3.2 Next as monuments of Tradition come *the Liturgy and sacred iconography*. The Liturgy, as the most intimate expression of Tradition, in the relations revelation sets up between, on the one hand, the Church-Bride and, on the other, her Spouse, the Church's Lord, is rich enough in revelatory content to suffice largely by itself to teach the faith—as often it does among the Eastern churches. The Liturgy centres on the celebration of the Covenant, the Paschal Mystery, to which in the "temporal cycle" (starting, for the Latin Church, in Advent) its whole year builds up. The heart of the Liturgy is the Mass, the Holy Sacrifice, anticipated at the Last Supper, offered on the Cross, and accepted by the Father at the Resurrection, to stunningly Pentecostal effect. But the Liturgy never separates the Body from the Head, hence the "sanctoral cycle": the celebration of all the saints, for the whole mystical vine is here. A theological student must be well-versed in his own liturgical tradition, and also know something of others, within the East-West family of the Catholic Church as a whole.

4.3.3 *The creeds and councils* are interrelated topics, since while the creeds first formulated by the patristic Church derive from the liturgies of Baptism, such creeds achieved more dogmatically full form through the work of the ecumenical councils. This linkage of creeds and councils is a happy one, because both creeds and councils belong with the "communion" nature of the Church as bearer of the Gospel. The Church is a communion of life in the Holy Trinity, of which the gateway is the act of faith in the Trinity's being and action as summed up in the creeds. And she is that same communion as a people gathered around the apostles in their successors, the bishops, who are the principal teachers of the churches, above all when they come together in councils either convoked or at least recognized by the one bishop who is the personal successor to the chief of the apostles, Saint Peter. The creeds have a further extension in subsequent doctrinal determinations made by the bishops with the pope in later councils, or by the pope alone when he teaches *ex cathedra*, "from the chair [of Peter]". And likewise the councils have a further resonance when the bishops, acting in their own local churches of which they are the chief pastors, interpret the apostolic deposit through putting forth theses in matters of faith and morals "to be held definitively" by all the faithful, and do so by a common voice that *echoes or at least is echoed by* the "Petrine" voice of the bishop of Rome, "Peter". Creeds and councils, and their extensions thus understood, are also forms in which Tradition comes to us.

4.3.4 So too are the *lives of the saints and popular piety* when understood as expressions of the *sensus fidelium*, "the sense of the faithful". Tradition is both preserved and transmitted by the actions in which the faithful (of whom by far the larger portion are the lay faithful), especially the most ardent of them—that is, the most devoted to the love of God and neighbor—turn into practice the faith of the Church. Their *pietas*, which attunes them to the revelatory deposit, is shown not only in their moral life, liturgical practice, and devotional exercises, but also in a wide range of further mediations, in contributions to education, art, and other cultural creations, philosophy, and scholarship, and all founding or sustaining of institutions that help transform the human city into a nearer approximation to the City of God. The saints, like the most devoted of the faithful, taken in the great historical spectrum of their activity, have excelled in all of these, thus constituting their own lives, whether in their entirety or in segments of their acting, further monuments of Tradition in which the Gospel comes to expression in illumination of the biblical word.

4.4 Before leaving the topic of the sources, Scripture and Tradition, consideration must also be given to two *aids to discernment* in scanning those sources. There are two of these: Christian experience and the nondefinitive teaching of the contemporary Magisterium.

4.4.1 All *Christian experience* that is not distorted by extrarevelatory factors of a kind incompatible with the created wisdom (see chapter 2) derives from and leads into the *sensus fidei*, "the sense of the faith". While its highest reach is found in mystical experience in the full sense, it is found wherever there is attunement to the mysteries, the realities of faith, through the exercise of an anointed imagination, a sensibility seriously affected by the grace of faith.

4.4.2 The contemporary *Magisterium*, acting in a nondefinitive but still "authentic" (that is, authoritative) manner, has the right to judge the deliverances of Christian experience so understood, precisely by submitting its claims to the test of theological wisdom. The chief task of the Magisterium, in the service of the Word, is to protect the primal form against distortion in one or more of its aspects. So, definition is not its chief task but an extraordinary one, the *ultima ratio* of its existence. Magisterial interventions may thus be admonitory rather than decisive. Yet, these two are linked because a further step may be needed so as to keep the deposit safe. Thus, errors provoked by distortions of experience—when a person or group of persons departs *either* from created wisdom (naturally, through false inferences from experience in morals or philosophy), *or* from the revealed expression of the Uncreated Wisdom (supernaturally, through inferences from experience that lack congruence with the apostolic deposit)—may, after a process of magisterial discernment, stimulate a "development of doctrine" in the universal Church. Alas, theologians are not immune to such errors, and like the heresiarchs of the past they can be irritants that encourage oysters to produce pearls. Here, however, care must be taken. What is meant by the development of doctrine is the reflective unfolding of depths of truth that are not new to the Church but already tacitly present, since the fullness of saving truth (short of the final Parousia) has been given apostolically. Still, "in the divine-human conscience of the Church, insofar as it includes temporality and relativity this fullness enters only successively and partially"—or dogma would have no history at all.[3]

[3] Sergei Bulgakov, "Dogma and Dogmatic Theology", in *Tradition Alive*, ed. Michael Plekon (Lanham, MD: Bowman and Littlefield, 2003), p. 76.

5

The Subject Matters of Theology

5.1 By such "subject matters" is understood the *various specializations* that the once unitary body of theology gave rise to over the course of time, and notably in the early modern period (sixteenth to eighteenth centuries).

5.1.1 It has been characteristic of theology since the early modern era to develop more and more specializations, like a tree putting out fresh branches. One might think in this connexion of the Baroque era's love for complex artistic virtuosity or the nineteenth century's habit of extending evolutionary ways of thinking to anything and everything. The *emergence of specialized theological treatises or tractates* that divided up the subject matter of theology between them had pedagogical advantages, especially as the sheer volume of historical data available to the student (or teacher) became less manageable, owing to the development of patristic and biblical study. That process of the ever-greater specialization of theology's ancillary disciplines continued in the twentieth century, owing not least to the movements of *ressourcement* which continued to amplify relevant factual knowledge in the areas of biblical exegesis, patristics, liturgics, and historical theology generally.

5.1.2 But in the twentieth century there has been something of a contrary process: the *contraction of complexity* in inherited Catholicism by means of a focussed simplicity. The description of the convergence method in chapter 3 suggests how this might be done without loss of doctrinal richness and consequent neglect of facets of the apostolic deposit. Von Balthasar was outstanding in seeking to show how the diversity of theological disciplines (and, even more taxingly, of theological writers) could be turned into a symphony played by a well-schooled orchestra,[1] though his understanding of totality thinking

---

[1] See Hans Urs von Balthasar, *Truth Is Symphonic* (San Francisco: Ignatius Press, 1987).

undervalued the desirability of systematics in the "circular" sense given to that term in chapter 2. Overall, however, it remains unlikely that separate treatises in theology will ever completely disappear, and indeed the Canadian Jesuit Bernard Lonergan has sought to supply for them a theoretical justification going beyond the demands of mere convenience.[2] The principal such subdivisions of theology found in the contemporary period are as follows.

5.1.3 As its name suggests, *fundamental theology* should be mentioned before the rest. It has two tasks: to establish the foundations of the act of faith, and to identify the criteria for theologically appropriate statements in systematic or speculative dogmatics.

5.1.3.1 In its first role, *establishing the foundations of the act of faith*, fundamental theology will make considerable use of philosophy, since philosophy is crucial to the preamble of faith, notably on the questions of how the divine might be said to open itself to communication with the human,

---

[2] See Bernard Lonergan, S.J., *Method in Theology* (New York: Crossroad, 1972), pp. 125–45.

and the human being to receive communication from the divine, should it be offered. In looking at the evidences for a revelation in history, fundamental theology can expect to make use of a range of tools for investigating Scripture, including those honed for use in the study of noninspired writing. But it will also want to present the wider claim found in the existence of the Church as occasioned by the Resurrection of Christ—since this claim makes the difference between a purely personal interpretation of the biblical signs and a fully evangelical one. Evidently, in this first role fundamental theology is closely akin to the apologetics or "dialectical theology" generated by the *prima theologia* of the doxologically contemplative theology described in chapter 3. Fundamental theology has in common with apologetics the justification of revelation as such.

5.1.3.2 The second role of fundamental theology is to lay out *the criteria theology will use when it applies itself to the disciplined exploration of revelation's contents* rather than to the justification of revelation's claims. Here it will enquire into the divine authority of Scripture and Tradition, the nature of biblical inspiration, the weight to be accorded to the different monuments of Tradition, the scope of revelation as its emerges from the sources, its centering in the mysteries of Christ, and its interpretation by reference not only to the sources but to the aids of discernment found in Christian experience and the guidance of the contemporary Magisterium.

5.1.4 *Dogmatic* theology comes in two forms: historical or positive theology, and systematic or speculative theology.

5.1.4.1 Considered as *historical theology*, dogmatics includes biblical exegesis when the latter is practised according to the ecclesial approach described in chapter 4. Dogmatics seen as positive theology will pay especial attention to the patristic era, as the moment when the biblical revelation was holistically registered in the postapostolic Church. It will also enquire into the contribution of the postpatristic Doctors, notably Saint Thomas, who has received the title *Doctor communis* for his ability to synthesise the teachings of the Fathers both with each other and with the *philosophia perennis*. A comparable function is played in the Christian East by Saint Maximus the Confessor and (especially)

Saint John Damascene, whose achievements are entitled, accordingly, to especial weight.[3] Positive theology does not, in fact, exclude any period as unworthy of study, since in every century Catholic divines have had things to say that are capable of throwing light on the revelatory "given".

5.1.4.2 Dogmatic theology in its *systematic* or speculative mode will not content itself with amassing informational data in the manner of positive theology. Instead, it will want to make use of these data in devising an architectonic whole in which they can put forth their full didactic power in revelation's service. Dogmatics understood as systematic or speculative theology will employ for this purpose the (superordinate) theological principle of order and the (subordinate) philosophical principle of order, set out, with illustrative examples, in chapter 3.

5.1.5 *Moral* theology concerns itself with the ethical action of Christians. Insofar as morals shares

[3] See Aidan Nichols, O.P., *Byzantine Gospel: Maximus the Confessor in Modern Scholarship* (Edinburgh: T&T Clark, 1993); Andrew Louth, *St. John Damascene: Tradition and Originality in Byzantine Tradition* (Oxford: Oxford University Press, 2002).

in the wisdom character of right philosophy, it will present human living in the light of its goal, which objectively is the good and subjectively is happiness or natural beatitude, as well as the means to that goal which are the virtues whereby man flourishes. Insofar as morals can be called the science of action, it generates its own principles—the precepts of the moral law, but since action is always singular and attended by circumstance, the principles of morality must be applied by conscience and prudence. Moral theology integrates such ethical discussion, but it goes further for it concerns the specifically Christian moral life. Its excess compared with ethics mirrors the way in which theological wisdom, based on supernatural revelation, transcends the philosophical wisdom that derives from natural philosophy (see chapter 3). In the Church, the Gospel community, moral action and spiritual life are unified, and the precepts of the natural law are exceeded in scope by the Beatitudes of the Sermon on the Mount, just as the natural virtues are exceeded in range likewise by the infused moral virtues and the theological virtues of faith, hope, and charity. This "excess" in the distinctively Christian moral life is closely connected with the sending of the Holy Spirit as the interiorized "law" (called such only by analogy) of the New Covenant. It takes its highest form under the influence of the gifts of the Holy Spirit, which render human action spontaneously docile to divine invitation, thus paralleling in the moral realm the greater value of the "wisdom of the saints" in the theological realm, through infused Wisdom (see chapter 2). The Church's traditional exegesis includes what the French Jesuit theologian Henri de Lubac called a "mystical tropology" (from the Greek *tropos*, meaning "to do with behaviour").[4] As between Christian morals and Christian mysticism there is a shared appropriation of God's saving work in the mysteries of Christ, notably in the Paschal Mystery, which is the fount of the Spirit's outpouring. This combination of moral and mystical values constitutes *spirituality*, which characteristically offers a programme for the maturation of the personality under grace. When treated as a development from initial conversion to transforming union with God (*theosis*), the content of spirituality may be laid out as a movement

[4] William F. Murphy Jr., "Henri de Lubac's Mystical Tropology", *Communio* 27:1 (2000): 171–201.

from a primarily ascetical phrase of Christian living to one where the mystical dimension increasingly predominates through the liberating possession of the self by the Holy Trinity as operative through the mysteries of Christ. That generates the pairing of terms whereby spirituality may be termed a combination of "ascetical and mystical theology".

5.1.6 *Practical theology* may be regarded as synonymous with pastoral theology in the *wider* sense of the latter phrase. The *narrower* sense of *pastoral theology* is confined to reflection on what is needed for the ministry of the Word and sacraments, and for pastoral care of the faithful (including those with special difficulties) on the part of the ordained. But throughout the Church's fellowship, and going beyond the typical tasks of ministry, the anointed imagination at work in Christian experience finds expression in a variety of practical ways like education, pro-life activity, social service (notably to the poor and marginalized), and participation in the communications media with its opportunities for mission, as well as in that production of Christian art and literature which the phrase "anointed imagination" may more immediately connote. Practical theology studies how in such multiform *Christian practice* the world is brought closer to its eschatological goal.

CONCLUSION

As already flagged in the above initial overview, this conclusion aims to translate the set of *objective* features, which, taken together, make up the theologian's project, into the terms of a series of *subjective* qualities which he will need to develop in order to make this project a success.

From chapter 1, where I asked "What Is Theology?", it emerges that the theologian must have the capacity to draw conceptual distinctions—distinctions not simply between things but also between ideas. Is one idea coherent with another? Does it contain any internal contradiction? Not for nothing was logical studies a major part of the "liberal arts" formation of the learner theologian of the High Middle Ages. However well-intentioned the would-be theologian may be in other respects, without this most basic of intellectual gifts he would be better advised not to start out on the journey. But chapter 1 also indicated another, very different, quality of mind (and heart) without which theology is altogether impossible. The theologian must have received the gift of supernatural faith. He is not a philosopher of religion, or a practitioner of "religious studies": a discipline for which agnosticism or indeed atheism would not disqualify the student. Only someone whose mind and heart have been moved to make the act of faith in the historically given divine revelation centred on Christ and transmitted in the Church by his Spirit can ever hope to be a theologian. These two qualities—the ability to make conceptual distinctions, on the one hand, and, on the other, supernatural faith—may seem an oddly assorted duo. But far from it! The capacity to distinguish the supernatural revelation found in the ecclesial community from the natural revelation found in the world around us is the first of the necessary conceptual distinctions the theologian must make.

From chapter 2, where the topic under discussion was "Theology as Science and Wisdom", further subjective requirements step into the light. The "scientific" demands placed by theology on the would-be practitioner entail two distinct qualities of mind. Firstly, the theologian must be able to grasp not just conceptual distinctions in general but more especially that subset of conceptual distinctions which the great Scholastic teachers termed "formal distinctions", for concepts need to be deployed in a

variety of different perspectives in order to bring out
the multiple aspects of things, actions, and events.
The formal perspective which governs theology
is the aspect of the relationship of all these to the
mystery of God and his saving design. But secondly,
the theologian has to develop the ingenuity required
to interrelate the relevant things, actions, and events
he is studying in this formal perspective not only to
God but also to each other. Here, the maxim "Only
connect!" gives theologians their watchword.

Then there are the "sapiential" or wisdom
demands of the theological enterprise. The theologian must become wise—and, as chapter 2 showed,
the wisdom needed is threefold. The theologian
must be judicious in his use of philosophy. He must
become profound in his penetration of his theological subject matter. And he must show distinct signs
of acquiring a touch of that wisdom of the saints
whereby, through sanctifying grace and the gifts
of the Holy Spirit, they enjoy even now a taste of
the realities of which theology speaks. The theologian must be intent, then, on a life of holiness, not
least through that most direct medium of such a life
which is prayer. He must be willing to be taught by
the sacred Liturgy, which has the capacity to form
his mind and heart in all the dispositions that belong
to the Gospel, and to open himself to the wonder

which is the beauty of the Christian mystery the Liturgy sets before him. Only so is he likely to strike the right balance between "cataphatic" or affirmative and "apophatic" or negative theology: to know where to locate the boundary line between that of which we can speak and that where we had better remain in an awed silence.

Chapter 3, in which I considered "Theological Principles and Methods", also set the theological practitioner something of a challenge. From the previous chapter it had emerged that theology as a science requires the ability to make formal distinctions and to organize the formally distinct material by interconnecting its constituent parts. Yet, so chapter 3 insisted, this cannot be done without deploying some principle of selection which will convey a vision of natural reality at large (a *philosophical principle of order*) and a vision of reality as supernaturally disclosed in particular (a *theological principle of order*). Here is where the theologian must nourish the gift of imagination. I use the word in the sense of that power which enables us to produce an architectonic—or overall—vision of the world.

The methods the theologian must learn to use, as laid out in chapter 3, will assist him in this heroic task. Practising the "analogy of being" will sensitivise him to the transcendentals, those universal qualities of being that point most directly to God. Practising the "analogy of faith" will deepen, in a way proper to supernatural revelation, the capacity to connect. Practising "totality thinking" will encourage the mind to take wing in pursuit of its architectonic goal. Practising the "method of convergence" will ensure that the architectonic scheme genuinely draws together to their rightful centre all the contributions that Christian doctrine can make to the total picture.

Chapter 4, which looked at the "Sources of Theology", stretches the ability of the theological student to cope with "information overload". He must develop his memory power to absorb as much of the Bible as he can, bearing in mind that not only the work of historical scholars but also the comments of the Church Fathers on the Scriptures are germane to his task. Indeed, for any interconnected and ultimately architectonic reading of the Bible the Fathers will often be more useful to him than the specialist exegetes. Mention of the Fathers leads on naturally to another enormous area of information: the many "monuments" in which Tradition's reading of Scripture—and the apostolically carried revelation more widely—has been embodied over time. The theological student must have some familiarity with the writings of the Fathers; with the Liturgies of East and West—but especially his own—and with iconography; with the teachings of the councils and the—rather small number of—*ex cathedra* pronouncements of the popes; and with the lives of the saints and the practices of popular piety.

Fortunately, he can run this huge quantity of factual material through the sieve of his own Christian experience, which, if it is functioning as it should, will sensitivise him to what is more important and what is less. Furthermore, in addition to this "aid to discernment" the theologian has a second available, and that is the way these variegated materials are either expounded or presumed in the teaching of the contemporary Magisterium. In the early twenty-first century that will mean above all the great *Catechism of the Catholic Church* promulgated by Pope Saint John Paul II in 1992.[1]

Lastly, chapter 5 described the "Subject Matters of Theology" as these have come to exist in academic faculties or seminaries in the contemporary period. The increasing specialization of theology, caused by its growing internal differentiation since the late mediaeval period, also has demands to make. Reading copiously must be something

[1] *Catechism of the Catholic Church*, 2nd ed. (Washington, DC: Libreria Editrice Vaticana–United States Catholic Conference, 1994, 1997, 2000).

the theological student is entirely happy to do.
But if the theological learner is cast down at this
prospect, let him take courage. The value of the
current theological specializations rests in the end
on their capacity to contribute to the remaking in
an enriched form of a classical theology where, as
with the High Scholastics of the thirteenth century,
all the most vital theological materials can be
accessed within the "limits" of a single comprehensive work.

May the blessing of God and the prayers of the holy
Doctors accompany your work!

BIBLIOGRAPHY

A. General

A Catholic Dictionary of Theology. 3 vols. London: Nelson, 1962–1971 (unfinished).

The Catholic Encyclopaedia. 15 vols. London: Caxton, 1907–1912.

Cross, F. L., and E. A. Livingstone, eds. *The Oxford Dictionary of the Christian Church*. 3rd ed. Oxford: Oxford University Press, 1997.

Komonchak, Joseph, Mary Collins, and Dermot A. Lane, eds. *The New Dictionary of Theology*. Dublin: Gill and Macmillan, 1987.

The New Catholic Encyclopaedia. 16 vols. 2 suppl. vols. New York: McGraw-Hill, 1967–1974.

O'Collins, Gerald, S.J., and Edward G. Farrugia, S.J. *A Concise Dictionary of Theology*. New York: Paulist, 1991.

Rahner, Karl, S.J., ed. *Encyclopaedia of Theology: A Concise Sacramentum Mundi*. London: Burns and Oates, 1975.

———, ed. *Sacramentum Mundi: An Encyclopaedia of Theology*. 6 vols. New York: Herder and Herder, 1968–1970.

Ratzinger, Joseph. *The Nature and Mission of Theology*. San Francisco: Ignatius Press, 1995.

B. Particular

Chapter 1: What Is Theology?

Natural revelation

Daniélou, Jean. *God and the Ways of Knowing*. Cleveland: Meridian, 1962.

Donceel, Joseph Florent. *Natural Theology*. New York: Sheed and Ward, 1963.

Hemming, Laurence Paul, and Susan Parsons, eds. *Restoring Faith in Reason*. London: Student Christian Movement, 2002.

Hütter, Reinhold, and Paul Griffiths, eds. *Reason and the Reasons of Faith*. Edinburgh: T&T Clark, 2005.

Jolivet, Régis. *The God of Reason*. London: Burns and Oates, 1959.

Nichols, Aidan, O.P. *From Hermes to Benedict XVI: Faith and Reason in Modern Catholic Thought*. Leominster: Gracewing, 2009.

Rahner, Karl, S.J. *Hearer of the Word: Laying the Foundation for a Philosophy of Religion*. New York: Continuum, 1994.

———. "Philosophy and Theology". In *Theological Investigations*, 6:71–81. London: Darton, Longman, and Todd, 1969.

Boersma, Hans. *Nouvelle Théologie and Sacramental Ontology: A Return to Mystery*. Oxford: Oxford University Press, 2005.

Bouillard, Henri. *The Logic of the Faith*. Dublin: Gill, 1967.

Guitton, Jean. *The Church and the Gospel*. London: Burns and Oates, 1961.

Latourelle, René, S.J. *Christ and the Church: Signs of Salvation*. New York: Alba House, 1972.

―――. *Theology of Revelation*. Slough: St. Paul's, 1966.

Marmion, Columba, O.S.B. *Christ in His Mysteries*. Bethesda, MD: Zacchaeus, 2008.

Persson, Per Erik. *Sacra Doctrina, Reason and Revelation in Aquinas*. Oxford: Basil Blackwell, 1970.

Rahner, Karl, S.J. "The Concept of Mystery in Catholic Theology". In *Theological Investigations*, 4:64–82. London: Darton, Longman, and Todd, 1966.

―――. *Foundations of Christian Faith*. London: Darton, Longman, and Todd, 1972.

Schillebeeckx, Edward, O.P. *Christ, the Sacrament of Encounter with God*. London: Sheed and Ward, 1963.

―――. *Revelation and Theology*. London: Sheed and Ward, 1967.

Sullivan, F. A., S.J. "The Theologian's Ecclesial Vocation and the 1990 CDF [Congregation for the Doctrine of the Faith] Instruction". *Theological Studies* 52 (1991): 51–68.

Von Balthasar, Hans Urs. *Explorations in Theology.* Vol. 1, *The Word Made Flesh.* San Francisco: Ignatius Press, 1989.

———. *Mysterium Paschale: The Mystery of Easter.* Edinburgh: T&T Clark, 1990.

———. *A Theological Anthropology.* New York: Sheed and Ward, 1967.

Chapter 2: Theology as Science and Wisdom

Theology as science

Chenu, Marie-Dominique, O.P. *Is Theology a Science?* London: Burns and Oates, 1959.

Latourelle, René. *Theology: Science of Salvation.* New York: Alba House, 1970.

O'Meara, Thomas F., O.P. *Church and Culture: German Catholic Theology, 1860–1914.* Notre Dame, IN: University of Notre Dame Press, 1991.

Van Ackeren, G. F., S.J. *Sacra Doctrina: The Subject of the First Question of the "Summa Theologiae" of St. Thomas Aquinas.* Rome: Catholic Book Agency, 1952.

Theology as wisdom

Cessario, Romanus, O.P. *Christian Faith and the Theological Life.* Washington, DC: Catholic University of America Press, 1996.

Louth, Andrew. *Discerning the Mystery: An Essay on the Nature of Theology*. Oxford: Clarendon Press, 1983.

Maritain, Jacques. *The Degrees of Knowledge*. London: Bles, 1937.

———. *Science and Wisdom*. London: Bles, 1940.

Mouroux, Jean. *I Believe: The Personal Structure of Faith*. London: Geoffrey Chapman, 1959.

Theology, holiness, contemplation

Brooke, Odo, O.S.B. *Studies in Monastic Theology*. Kalamazoo, MI: Cistercian Studies, 1980.

Gilson, Etienne. *The Mystical Theology of St. Bernard*. London: Sheed and Ward, 1940.

Leclerq, Jean, O.S.B. *The Love of Learning and the Desire for God*. 2nd ed. New York: Fordham University Press, 1974.

Merton, Thomas. *The Climate of Monastic Prayer*. Shannon: Irish University Press, 1969.

———. *The Monastic Journey*. Kalamazoo, MI: Cistercian Studies, 1977.

Von Balthasar, Hans Urs. "Theology and Holiness". In *Explorations in Theology*. Vol. 1, *The Word Made Flesh*, pp. 181–210. San Francisco: Ignatius Press, 1989.

Theology, the Liturgy, aesthetics

Casel, Odo, O.S.B. *The Mystery of Worship and Other Writings*. London: Newman, 1962.

Corbon, Jean. *The Wellspring of Worship*. San Francisco: Ignatius Press, 2005.

Hart, David Bentley. *The Beauty of the Infinite: The Aesthetics of Christian Truth*. Grand Rapids, MI: Eerdmans, 2007.

Von Balthasar, Hans Urs. *The Glory of the Lord: A Theological Aesthetics*. Vol. 1, *Seeing the Form*. Edinburgh: T&T Clark, 1982.

Cataphatic and apophatic

Lossky, Vladimir. *The Mystical Theology of the Eastern Church*. London: James Clarke, 1957.

Pieper, Josef. *The Silence of St. Thomas: Three Essays*. South Bend, IN: St. Augustine's Press, 1999.

Chapter 3: Theological Principles and Methods

Principles of order, philosophical and theological

Chenu, Marie-Dominique. *The Scope of the Summa Theologiae of St. Thomas*. Washington, DC: Thomist Press, 1958.

⸻. *Towards Understanding St. Thomas*. Chicago: Regnery, 1964.

Ernst, Harold E. "New Horizons in Catholic Philosophical Theology: *Fides et ratio* and the Changed Status of Thomism". *Heythrop Journal* 47 (2006): 26–37.

Gilson, Etienne. *The Christian Philosophy of St. Thomas Aquinas*. London: Victor Gollancz, 1957.

———. *Saint Thomas Aquinas*. London: British Academy, 1932.

Nichols, Aidan, O.P. *Chalice of God: A Systematic Theology in Outline*. Collegeville, MN: Liturgical Press, 2012.

———. *The Shape of Catholic Theology: An Introduction to Its Principles, Sources and History*. Collegeville, MN: Liturgical Press, 1991.

Sertillanges, Antonin-Dalmace, O.P. *Foundations of Thomistic Philosophy*. London: Sands, 1931.

Von Balthasar, Hans Urs. *The Truth Is Symphonic: Aspects of Christian Pluralism*. San Francisco: Ignatius Press, 1988.

Methods: analogy of being, analogy of faith, totality, convergence

Dulles, Avery, S.J. *The Craft of Theology: From Symbol to System*. Dublin: Gill and Macmillan, 1992.

Lamb, Matthew. *History, Method and Theology*. Missoula, MT: Scholars Press, 1978.

Lyttkens, Hampus. *The Analogy between God and the World: An Investigation of Its Background and Interpretation of Its Use by Thomas of Aquino*. Uppsala: Lundekvist, 1952.

Nichols, Aidan, O.P. *A Key to Balthasar: Hans Urs von Balthasar on Beauty, Goodness and Truth*. London: Darton, Longman and Todd, 2011.

Ratzinger, Joseph. *Principles of Catholic Theology: Building Stones for a Fundamental Theology.* San Francisco: Ignatius Press, 1987.

Von Balthasar, Hans Urs. *Convergences: To the Source of the Christian Mystery.* San Francisco: Ignatius Press, 1982.

————. *The Theology of Karl Barth.* San Francisco: Ignatius Press, 1992.

"Via anglica"

Coulson, John, and A. M. Allchin, eds. *The Rediscovery of Newman: An Oxford Symposium.* London: Sheed and Ward and Society for the Promotion of Christian Knowledge, 1967.

Walgrave, J. H., O.P. *Newman the Theologian: The Nature of Belief and Doctrine as Exemplified in His Life and Works.* London: Geoffrey Chapman, 1960.

Chapter 4: The Sources of Theology

Scripture

Abraham, J. W. *Divine Revelation and the Limits of Historical Criticism.* Oxford: Oxford University Press, 1982.

Daniélou, Jean, S.J. *The Bible and the Liturgy.* London: Darton, Longman, and Todd, 1960.

————. *From Shadows to Reality: Studies in the Biblical Typology of the Fathers.* London: Burns and Oates, 1960.

De Lubac, Henri, S.J. *Scripture in the Tradition*. New York: Crossroad, 2001.

De Margerie, Bertrand. *An Introduction to the History of Exegesis*. Petersham, MA: St. Bede's Publications, 1994–1995.

Farkasfalvy, Denis, O. Cist. *Inspiration and Interpretation: A Theological Introduction to Sacred Scripture*. Washington, DC: Catholic University of America Press, 2010.

Grelot, Pierre. "Relations between the Old and New Testament in Jesus Christ". In *Problems and Perspectives of Fundamental Theology*, edited by René Latourelle, S.J., and Gerald O'Collins, S.J., pp. 186–205. New York: Paulist, 1982.

Marrow, Stanley B. *Basic Tools of Biblical Exegesis*. 2nd ed. Rome: Pontifical Biblical Institute, 1978.

Rahner, Karl, S.J. *Inspiration in the Bible*. New York: Herder, 1966.

Robinson, Robert Bruce. *Roman Catholic Exegesis since "Divino afflante Spiritu"*. Atlanta: Scholars Press, 1988.

Valkenburg, W. G. B. M. *Words of the Living God: Place and Function of Holy Scripture in the Theology of St. Thomas Aquinas*. Louvain: Peeters, 2000.

Tradition

Congar, Yves. *The Meaning of Tradition*. San Francisco: Ignatius Press, 2004.

─────. *Tradition and Traditions: An Historical and a Theological Essay*. London: Burns and Oates, 1966.

Rahner, Karl, S.J., and Joseph Ratzinger. *Revelation and Tradition*. New York: Herder and Herder, 1966.

The Fathers and Doctors

Bettenson, Henry, ed. *The Early Christian Fathers: A Selection from the Writings of the Fathers from St. Clement of Rome to St. Athanasius*. Oxford: Oxford University Press, 1969.

─────. *The Later Christian Fathers: A Selection from the Writings of the Fathers from St. Cyril of Jerusalem to St. Leo the Great*. Oxford: Oxford University Press, 1972.

Daley, Brian, S.J. "The Nouvelle Théologie and the Patristic Revival: Sources, Symbols and the Science of Theology". *International Journal of Scientific Theology* 7 (2005): 362–82.

Drobner, Hubertus. *The Fathers of the Church: A Comprehensive Introduction*. Peabody, MA: Hendrickson, 2007.

McGinn, Bernard. *The Doctors of the Church: Twenty-Three Men and Women Who Shaped the Church*. New York: Crossroad, 1999.

Ramsey, Boniface, O.P. *Beginning to Read the Fathers*. London: Darton, Longman, and Todd, 1985.

Turner, Henry Ernest William. *The Pattern of Christian Truth: A Study in the Relations between*

Orthodoxy and Heresy in the Early Church. London: Mowbray, 1954.

The liturgies and sacred art

Nichols, Aidan, O.P. *Redeeming Beauty: Essays in Sacral Aesthetics.* Aldershot: Ashgate, 2007.

Ouspensky, Leonide, and Vladimir Lossky. *The Meaning of Icons.* Crestwood, NY: St. Vladimir's Seminary Press, 1982.

Vagaggini, Cipriano, O.S.B. *Theological Dimensions of the Liturgy.* Collegeville, MN: Liturgical Press, 1976.

Creeds and councils

De Lubac, Henri, S.J. *The Christian Faith: An Essay on the Structure of the Apostles' Creed.* San Francisco: Ignatius Press, 1988.

Dvornik, Francis. *The Ecumenical Councils.* New York: Hawthorne, 1961.

Kelly, J. N. D. *Early Christian Creeds.* 3rd ed. London: Longmans, Green, 1976.

Lamb, Matthew, and Matthew Levering, eds. *Vatican II: Renewal within Tradition.* New York: Oxford University Press, 2008.

The "sense of the faithful"

Newman, John Henry. *On Consulting the Faithful in Matters of Doctrine.* Edited by John Coulson. London: Geoffrey Chapman, 1961.

Aids to discernment

DiNoia, J. Augustine, O.P. "Authority, Public Dissent, and the Nature of Theological Thinking". *Thomist* 52 (1988): 185–301.

Dulles, Avery. *Magisterium: Teacher and Guardian of the Faith*. Naples, FL: Sapientia Press, 2008.

Mouroux, Jean. *Christian Experience: An Introduction to Theology*. London: Sheed and Ward, 1954.

Nichols, Aidan, O.P. *From Newman to Congar: The Idea of Doctrinal Development from the Victorians to the Second Vatican Council*. Edinburgh: T&T Clark, 1990.

Sullivan, Francis A., S.J. *Magisterium: Teaching Authority in the Catholic Church*. Dublin: Gill and Macmillan, 1983.

Walgrave, Jan Hendrik. *Unfolding Revelation: The Nature of Doctrinal Development*. London: Hutchinson, 1972.

Chapter 5: The Subject Matters of Theology

The emergence of theological
specialisation and its defence

Congar, Yves. *A History of Theology*. Garden City, NY: Doubleday, 1968.

Lonergan, Bernard, S.J. *Method in Theology*. New York: Crossroad, 1972.

Fundamental theology

Crehan, Joseph, S.J. "Apologetics". In *A Catholic Dictionary of Theology*, 1:113–22. London: Nelson, 1962.

Dulles, Avery, S.J. *A History of Apologetics*. Rev. ed. San Francisco: Ignatius Press, 2005.

Latourelle, René, S.J., and Rino Fisichella, eds. *Dictionary of Fundamental Theology*. Slough: St. Paul's, 1994.

O'Collins, Gerald, S.J. *Fundamental Theology*. London: Darton, Longman, and Todd, 1981.

Dogmatic theology

Aquinas, Thomas. *Light of Faith: The Compendium of Theology*. Manchester, NH: Sophia Institute Press, 1993.

Bulgakov, Sergei. "Dogma and Dogmatic Theology". In *Tradition Alive*, edited by Michael Plekon, pp. 67–80. Lanham, MD: Bowman and Littlefield, 2003.

Fiorenza, Francis Schüssler, and John P. Galvin, eds. *Systematic Theology: Roman Catholic Perspectives*. Dublin: Gill and Macmillan, 1991.

Kasper, Walter. *The Methods of Dogmatic Theology*. Shannon: Irish University Press, 1969.

McDermott, Timothy, ed. *St. Thomas Aquinas, Summa Theologiae: A Concise Translation*. London: Eyre and Spottiswoode, 1989.

Scheeben, Matthias Joseph. *The Mysteries of Christianity*. St. Louis, MO: Herder, 1946.

Moral theology

Cessario, Romanus, O.P. *The Moral Virtues and Theological Ethics*. Notre Dame, IN: Notre Dame University Press, 1991.
Pinckaers, Servais, O.P. *The Sources of Christian Ethics*. Washington, DC: Catholic University of America Press, 1998.

Practical theology

Carrier, Hervé. *Gospel Message and Human Cultures: From Leo XIII to John Paul II*. Pittsburgh: Duquesne University Press, 1989.
Milbank, J. *Theology and Social Theory: Beyond Secular Reason*. Oxford: Basil Blackwell, 1990.
Nichols, A. *Christendom Awake: On Re-energizing the Church in Culture*. Edinburgh: T&T Clark, 1999.
Rahner, Karl, S.J. *Mission and Grace*. 3 vols. London: Sheed and Ward, 1963–1966.